Anonymous

Meeting of Adjourned Conference of Bishops of the Anglican Communion

Holden at Lambeth Palace, December 10, 1867

Anonymous

Meeting of Adjourned Conference of Bishops of the Anglican Communion
Holden at Lambeth Palace, December 10, 1867

ISBN/EAN: 9783337067663

Printed in Europe, USA, Canada, Australia, Japan

Cover: Foto ©ninafisch / pixelio.de

More available books at **www.hansebooks.com**

MEETING

OF

Adjourned Conference of Bishops of the Anglican Communion,

HOLDEN AT LAMBETH PALACE, DECEMBER 10, 1867.

I.—REPORTS OF COMMITTEES APPOINTED BY THE CONFERENCE.

II.—RESOLUTIONS OF THE ADJOURNED CON-FERENCE.

PUBLISHED BY AUTHORITY.

London,

RIVINGTONS, WATERLOO PLACE;

HIGH STREET, | TRINITY STREET,
Oxford. | Cambridge.

1867.

REPORTS OF COMMITTEES APPOINTED BY THE CONFERENCE.

I.

REPORT of the Committee appointed under Resolution V., by the Conference of Bishops of the Anglican Communion, held at Lambeth Palace, September 24—27th, 1867[1].

The subject of the functions and relations of the several Synods, on which the Committee is ap-

---

[1] RESOLUTION IV.—" That, in the opinion of this Conference, Unity in Faith and Discipline will be best maintained among the several branches of the Anglican Communion by due and canonical subordination of the Synods of the several branches to the higher authority of a Synod or Synods above them."

RESOLUTION V.—" That a Committee of seven members (with power to add to their number, and to obtain the assistance of men learned in Ecclesiastical and Canon Law) be appointed to inquire into and report upon the subject of the relations and functions of such Synods, and that such Report be forwarded to his Grace the Lord Archbishop of Canterbury, with a request that, if possible, it may be communicated to any adjourned meeting of this Conference."

pointed to report, appears to them to be necessarily connected with questions as to the constitution of these bodies. The following Report, therefore, embraces the whole subject of Synods. In discussing it, your Committee deems it necessary to deal with the question in the abstract, without reference to existing laws and usages in the several branches of the Anglican Communion, and to lay down general principles, the adoption or application of which must depend on circumstances, such, for example, as the laws which any Church may have inherited or already established.

I.—In the organization of Synodal order for the government of the Church, the Diocesan Synod appears to be the primary and simplest form of such organization.

By the Diocesan Synod the co-operation of all members of the body is obtained in Church action; and that acceptance of Church rules is secured, which, in the absence of other law, usage, or enactment, gives to these rules the force of laws "binding on those who, expressly or by implication, have consented to them[2]."

For this reason, wherever the Church is not established by law, it is, in the judgment of your Committee, essential to order and good government that the Diocese should be organized by a Synod.

---

[2] Judgment of Judicial Committee of Privy Council in case of Long v. Bishop of Capetown. 1 Moore, P. C. C., N.S. 461.

Your Committee consider that it is not at variance with the ancient principles of the Church, that both Clergy and Laity should attend the Diocesan Synod, and that it is expedient that the Synod should consist of the Bishop and Clergy of the Diocese, with Representatives of the Laity.

The constitution of the Diocesan Synod may be determined either by rules for that branch of the Church established by the Synod of the Province, or by general consent in the Diocese itself, its rules being sanctioned afterwards by the Provincial Synod.

Your Committee, however, recommend that the following general rules should be adopted; viz., that the Bishop, Clergy, and Laity should sit together, the Bishop presiding; that votes should be taken by orders, whenever demanded; and that the concurrent assent of Bishop, Clergy, and Laity should be necessary to the validity of all acts of the Synod.

They consider that the Clerical members of the Synod should be those Clergy who are recognized by the Bishop, according to the rules of the Church in that Diocese, as being under his jurisdiction. Whether in large Dioceses, when the Clergy are very numerous, they might appear by representation, is a difficult question, and one on which your Committee are not prepared to express an opinion.

The Lay Representatives in the Synod ought,

in the judgment of your Committee, to be Male
Communicants of at least one year's standing in
the Diocese, and of the full age of twenty-one.   It
should be required that the electors should be
Members of the Church in that Diocese, and belong
to the parish in which they claim to vote.   It
appears desirable that the regular meetings of the
Synod should be fixed and periodical; but that
the right of convening special meetings whenever
they may be required should be reserved to the
Bishop.

The office of the Diocesan Synod is, generally,
to make regulations, not repugnant to those of
higher Synods, for the order and good government of the Church within the Diocese, and
to promulgate the decisions of the Provincial
Synod.

II.—The Provincial Synod—or, as it is called
in New Zealand, the General Synod, and in the
United States the General Convention—is formed,
whenever it does not exist already by law and
usage, through the voluntary association of Dioceses for united legislation and common action.
The Provincial Synod not only provides a method
for securing unity amongst the Dioceses which
are thus associated, but also forms the link between
these Dioceses and other Churches of the Anglican
Communion.

∗Without questioning the right of the Bishops
of any Province to meet in Synod by themselves,

and without affirming that the presence of others is essential to a Provincial Synod, your Committee recommend that, whenever no law or usage to the contrary already exists, it should consist of the Bishops of the Province, and of Representatives both of the Clergy and of the Laity in each Diocese. Your Committee need not define the method in which a Provincial Synod may be first constituted, but they assume that its constitution and rules will be determined by the concurrence of the several Dioceses duly represented.

Your Committee consider that it must be left to each Province to decide whether, and under what circumstances, the Bishops, Clergy, and Laity in a Provincial Synod should sit and discuss questions in the same chamber or separately; but, in the judgment of the Committee, the votes should in either case be taken by orders; and the concurrent assent of Bishops, Clergy, and Laity should be necessary for any legislative action, wherever the Clergy and Laity form part of the constitution of a Provincial Synod; such powers and functions not involving legislation being reserved as belong to the Bishops by virtue of their office.

The number, qualification, and mode of election of the Clerical and Lay Representatives from each Diocese must be determined by the Synods in the several Provinces.

It is the office of the Provincial Synod, generally, to exercise, within the limits of the Province, powers in regard to Provincial questions similar to those which the Diocesan Synod exercises, within the Diocese, in regard to Diocesan questions.

As to the relation between these two Synods, your Committee are of opinion that the Diocese is bound to accept positive enactments of a Provincial Synod in which it is duly represented, and that no Diocesan regulations have force, if contrary to the decisions of a higher Synod; but that, in order to prevent any collision or misunderstanding, the spheres of action of the several Synods should be defined on the following principle; viz., That the Provincial Synod should deal with questions of common interest to the whole Province, and with those which affect the communion of the Dioceses with one another and with the rest of the Church; whilst the Diocesan Synod should be left free to dispose of matters of local interest, and to manage the affairs of the Diocese.

From this principle your Committee draw the following conclusions :—

1. All alterations in the Services of the Church, required by circumstances in the Province, should be made or authorized by the Provincial Synod, and not merely by the Diocesan.

2. The rule of discipline for the Clergy of the Province should be framed by the Provincial Synod.

3. Rules for the trial of Clergy should be made by the Provincial Synod; but, in default of

such action on the part of that Synod, the Diocesan Synod should establish provisional rules for this purpose. The Provincial Tribunal of Appeal should be established by the Provincial Synod.

4. In questions relating to Patronage, the tenure of Church property, Parochial divisions, arrangements, officers, &c., there should be joint action of the Diocese and the Province; the former making such regulations as may be best suited to develope local resources, the latter providing against the admission of any principle inexpedient for the common interests of the Church.

5. The erection of a new Diocese within the limits of an existing Diocese should proceed by general rules established by the Provincial Synod.

6. The question of the election of a Bishop it is unnecessary here to consider, as it is submitted to another Committee.

III.—The question of a higher Synod of the Anglican Communion, and of the relation which the inferior Synods should hold towards it, whenever it might assemble, is one, your Committee are aware, of much greater difficulty than any of those which have been previously considered.

The fact, however, that a Conference of Bishops of the whole Anglican Communion has already met together, is of itself an indication of the need which is generally felt of united counsel in ·a sphere more extensive than that of a Provincial Synod. Indeed, the Resolutions under which this Committee was appointed contemplate the possibility at least of some Synod being established superior to the Provincial. It is also implied in Resolution VIII. of this Conference, that some such Assembly may be required, in order to preserve Colonial and Missionary Churches in close union with the Church of England, since it is provided that all changes in the Services of the Church made by one of their Provincial Synods should "be liable to revision by any Synod of the Anglican Communion in which the said Province should be represented."

The objections that may be urged against the united action of Churches which are more or less free to act independently, and other Churches whose constitution is fixed, not only by ancient ecclesiastical laws and usages but by the law of the State, are obvious; but it appears to your Committee that the action of this Conference has proved that the difficulties which are anticipated are not insuperable, and suggests the method by which they may be overcome. Under present circumstances, indeed, no Assembly that might be convened would be competent to enact canons of binding ecclesiastical authority on these different bodies, or to frame definitions of faith which it would be obligatory on the Churches of the Anglican Communion to accept. It would be necessary, therefore, in the judgment of your Committee, to avoid all terms respecting this

Assembly, that might imply authority of this nature, and to call it a Congress, if even the term Council should be considered open to objection. Its decisions could only possess the authority which might be derived from the moral weight of such united counsels and judgments, and from the voluntary acceptance of its conclusions by any of the Churches there represented.

Your Committee consider that his Grace the Archbishop of Canterbury, as occupying the See from which the Colonial and American Churches derive their succession, should be the convener of such an Assembly. That it should differ from the present Conference in being attended by both Clerical and Lay Representatives of the several Churches, as consultees and advisers, each Diocese being allowed to send, besides its Bishop, a presbyter and a lay member of the Church, if they should desire to be thus represented; and further, in the proceedings being more formal and, in part at least, public. The question when for the first time, and at what periods, this Congress or Council should be called, your Committee deem it more respectful to leave for the consideration of his Grace the Archbishop of Canterbury and of the present Conference.

G. A. NEW ZEALAND,
Chairman.

H. GRAHAMSTOWN,
Secretary.

II.

*REPORT of the Committee appointed under Re-
solution IX. of the Lambeth Conference, on the
Constitution of a voluntary spiritual Tribunal, to
which questions of Doctrine may be carried by
Appeal from the Tribunals for the exercise of discipline in each Province of the Colonial Church* [3].

After full consideration of objections that have
been urged against the establishment of any such
Tribunal as that contemplated by this Resolution,
your Committee are of opinion that these objections are not sufficient to outweigh the argu-
ments in its favour, and that most of the
objections will be found inapplicable to the particular form of Tribunal which the Committee
recommend.

Your Committee consider that such a Tribunal
is required in order to prevent the dissatisfaction
which would arise if important questions were
finally decided by those Colonial Churches, the

---

[3] RESOLUTION IX.—"That the Committee appointed by
Resolution V., with the addition of the names of the Bishops of
London, St. David's, and Oxford, and all the Colonial Bishops,
be instructed to consider the constitution of a voluntary spiritual Tribunal, to which questions of doctrine may be carried
by appeal from the Tribunals for the exercise of discipline in
each Province of the Colonial Church, and that their report be
forwarded to his Grace the Lord Archbishop of Canterbury,
who is requested to communicate it to an adjourned meeting of
this Conference."

circumstances of which render it impossible for them to form a sufficient Tribunal of last resort.

It would also tend to secure unity in matters of Faith, and uniformity in matters of Discipline, where Doctrine may be involved.

For these reasons your Committee recommend that such a Tribunal be established; and, from the desire expressed by several branches of the Colonial Church, that this should be one of the results of this Conference, they believe that it will be generally accepted by those for whose benefit it is designed.

At the same time, they are sensible of the great difficulty of forming such a Tribunal, and of the necessity of proceeding with caution, lest it should interfere with the liberties of the Colonial Churches, or should have any appearance of collision with the Courts established by law, either here or in Her Majesty's foreign possessions.

Your Committee now proceed to lay before the Conference their conclusions as to the functions and constitution of the proposed Tribunal.

They are of opinion that it should not take cognizance of any case which shall not have been referred to it by some branch of the Anglican Communion which has consented to its constitution. Thus it would not interfere either with those Churches in which provision is made by the State for the exercise of discipline, or with the liberty and rights of ecclesiastical Provinces.

These would be free to accept or to decline the appeal thus offered to them, and to withdraw afterwards their acceptance of the Tribunal, if they should so desire[4].

Your Committee consider that this Tribunal of Appeal should take into consideration all the facts of the case as sent up to it in writing from the inferior Tribunal; that the Appeal, however, should not be on the facts, but only on the points of Doctrine and Discipline involved in them.

That during the Appeal the sentence of the Provincial Tribunal should continue in force, so far as it affects the present exercise of spiritual functions by the accused.

That the judgments of the Tribunal of Appeal should be delivered in the form of a decision that the teaching or practice of the accused party is (or is not) permissible.

That the Tribunal should use as the standards of faith and doctrine by which its decisions shall be governed, those which are now in use in the United Church of England and Ireland; and that as to all matters not defined in such formularies, the judgments should be framed on any conclusions which shall be hereafter agreed to at any Council

---

[4] The decisions of such a Tribunal would be of the same nature as those of "arbitrators, whose jurisdiction rests entirely upon the agreement of the parties." (Judgment of Judicial Committee of the Privy Council in case of Long *v.* Bishop of Capetown, 1 Moore, P. C. C., N.S. 462.)

or Congress of the whole Anglican Communion : Provided always, that no such conclusion be contradictory to any now existing standard or formulary of the Church of England; and provided further, that the Synod of that Province of the Church from which the Appeal shall be sent, shall not have refused to accept such conclusion.

Your Committee further recommend, subject to any regulations that may be made at any future Conference of the Anglican Communion :—

That, as it is a Tribunal for decisions in matters of faith, Archbishops and Bishops only should be judges, his Grace the Lord Archbishop of Canterbury being the President.

That each Province in the Colonial Church should have the right of electing two members of the Tribunal; and that all the Dioceses of the Colonial Church not associated into Provinces should collectively have the right of electing two. That each Province of the United Church of England and Ireland should be requested to elect two members, but that the Province of Canterbury should elect three, in the event of his Grace the Archbishop not acting as President. That the Episcopal Church in Scotland should have the right of electing two. And (as it appears probable that the Protestant Episcopal Church in the United States would avail itself of such a Tribunal) that Church should have the right of electing five members.

In the judgment of the Committee, the Bishops of the several Churches should elect those who shall represent them on this tribunal.

That, so soon after January 1, 1869, as any ten names shall have been forwarded to the Archbishop of Canterbury as having been elected, the Tribunal should be deemed to be constituted.

That of the members thus elected, seven should form a quorum for the transaction of business, but a smaller number should have power to adjourn from time to time.

That the members of the Tribunal should continue in office, unless their seat be vacated by death, resignation, or removal by the electing body; but that, in the event of any Bishop of the Colonial or American Church notifying to the electing body that he is unable or declines to attend at any sitting of the Tribunal to which he may be summoned, it should be lawful for the body by which he was elected to appoint, instead of him, any Bishop of the Anglican Communion other than one of those already elected.

That, in the event of the Archbishop of Canterbury for the time being declining or being unable to act as President, it should be lawful for his Grace, if he should see fit, to nominate any other member of the Tribunal to act as President in his room; and in the event of no such appointment being made by him, that it should be lawful for the Tribunal at its first meeting to elect one of its members as President.

That the summons for the sitting of the Tribunal should be issued within thirty days from the time of the notice of Appeal being delivered by the agent of the Appellant to the proper officer of the Tribunal.

That the action of the Tribunal should not be impeded by the absence from it of any of those who are at liberty to sit in it, provided there be a quorum.

That, before the assembling of the Tribunal for the hearing of an Appeal, the President should nominate as Assessors three theologians and three persons learned in the law, who should be present at the trial, and should answer any questions as to theological learning and law put to them by the Tribunal through its President in writing, and who should be at liberty to tender in writing to the Tribunal through its President their opinion upon any point of theological learning or law which may arise, and that the Tribunal should be bound to consider such opinion before coming to its decision.

That parties before the Tribunal may be represented by any Counsel they may select, whether theologians or persons learned in the law.

That the rules of procedure of the said Tribunal, except as here provided for, should as far as possible be those of the higher Courts of Law, and that any necessary alterations in such rules should be made by the Tribunal itself.

That no sentence should be passed without the assent thereto of two-thirds of the Judges present during the trial.

That, at the time of delivering judgment, each member of the Tribunal who has been present during the trial should give his decision in writing, and may read or cause to be read openly in Court his decision, and the reasons for it; and that the judgment of the prescribed majority should be the judgment of the Tribunal.

F. MONTREAL,
Chairman.

H. GRAHAMSTOWN,
Secretary.

III.

On the Courts of Metropolitans, and the Trial of a Bishop or Metropolitan [5].

I.—Your Committee consider that the constitution of the Provincial Tribunal for Appeals from the decisions of Diocesan Tribunals should be determined, whenever it is not fixed by law, by the Synod of the Province; but it is expedient, in their judgment, that its rules should be assimilated, as far as circumstances will admit, to those of the proposed Tribunal of Appeal in England.

II.—In the case of charges against a Bishop, they suggest the following as general principles:—

That each Province should determine by rules made in its own Synod the offences for which a Bishop may be presented for trial, and who should be promoters of the charge.

That the charge should be presented to the Metropolitan.

That it appears doubtful whether a preliminary inquiry is expedient, provided that sufficient precautions are taken that no frivolous charges should be entertained.

That the Metropolitan should summon to the hearing of the cause all the Bishops of the Province (except the accused), who should sit as judges, not merely as assessors.

That no trial should take place, except before two-thirds of the Bishops of the Province, provided

Metropolitans, the Court of Metropolitans, the scheme for conducting the Election of Bishops, when not otherwise provided for, the declaration of submission to the Regulation of Synods, and the question of what Legislation should be proposed for the Colonial Churches, be referred to the Committee specified in the preceding Resolution."

that there be never fewer than three Bishops present, including the Metropolitan.

That if three Bishops of the Province should be unable to attend, it should be lawful for the Metropolitan to call in one or more Bishops not of the Province.

That it is desirable that, whenever it may be practicable, there should be Assessors, as recommended by this Committee for the higher Tribunal of Appeal.

That, in case of the non-appearance of the accused after sufficient citations, the trial may go forward as if he were present, or he may be punished for contumacy, according as the Province may prescribe.

That there should be no sentence except by the judgment of two-thirds of the Tribunal, or by three judges, whichever should be the greater number ; the assent of the Metropolitan not being necessary to the sentence.

That the general rules of procedure should be framed by the Synod of the Province; but should be, as far as possible, similar to those recommended by this Committee for the proposed Tribunal of Appeal.

That an appeal to the higher Tribunal recommended by this Committee should be allowed when the case is one of doctrine, or discipline involving doctrine, if notice of such appeal be given within   days from the delivery of sentence; and that, in all cases, proper provision should be made for a new trial on sufficient reason being shown.

That there should be no contract not to appeal to Civil Courts; but that sufficient provision should be made by the Declaration of Submission (to be considered in another Report), that the sentence of the Spiritual Tribunals may be effective.

That a Metropolitan should be tried in the same manner as any other Bishop—the senior Bishop, in that case, acting in the place of the Metropolitan.

F. MONTREAL,
Chairman.

H. GRAHAMSTOWN,
Secretary.

IV.

SCHEME for conducting the Election of Bishops, when not otherwise provided for.

Your Committee have to consider the proper mode for conducting the Election of a Bishop, wherever it is not provided for by any existing law, and without reference to any question -that might arise as to the temporalities connected with the see.

It is evident that there are two parties whose concurrent action is necessary in such an appointment; viz., the Clergy and Laity of the Diocese, and the Bishops of the Province by whom the person elected as Bishop is consecrated.

Your Committee are of opinion that, in accordance with the ancient usages of the Church, the election as a general rule should be made by the Diocese, and that the Bishops of the Province should confirm the election. They consider, however, that it is consistent with this principle that the Diocese should nominate two or more persons, of whom the Bishops of the Province should select one; or that the Diocese should delegate to any person or body the power of choosing a Bishop for the vacant see, it being understood that the Diocese must accept such choice as final.

The principle of the concurrent action of the two parties concerned would also be preserved if the Bishops of the Province should nominate two or more persons, from whom the Diocese should elect one.

In the election by the Diocese, it appears to your Committee that the right of selecting the person who shall be their Bishop belongs to the Clergy, the Laity having the right of accepting or rejecting the person so chosen. But it is expedient, in their judgment, that the election should always be made by the Diocesan Synod, wherever one is established, and in accordance with the rules of that Synod. In those Dioceses in which there is no Diocesan Synod, they recommend that, for the election of a Bishop, a Convention should be summoned by the Dean, senior Archdeacon, or senior Presbyter of the Diocese; that this Convention should consist of all Presbyters, and of Lay-representatives, who should be male communicants of at least twenty-one years of age; that these Representatives should be elected by each parish or congregation, in such manner as should be determined by the convener; that the person who should obtain the majority of votes of the Clergy, and also of those of the Lay-representatives, present at the Convention, should be accounted to be elected to the Bishopric; that this election should not be vitiated by the absence of any of the parties summoned, or by the failure of any congregation or parish to elect a Lay-representative; that any question as to the validity of the election to the vacant see should be submitted, prior to the Consecration, to the Consecrating Bishops, whose decision should be final; and that after the consecration of a Bishop no objection should be entertained.

They further recommend that, where the Diocese is included in a Province, the confirmation of an election should be by the Metropolitan and a majority of the Bishops of the Province; but where the Diocese is extra-provincial, that the confirmation should rest with the Archbishops of Canterbury and York, and the Bishop of London ; that the power of confirmation should be absolute— the Bishops having the right to refuse to confirm the election, without assigning any reason for their refusal.

All further rules necessary for conducting the election should, in the opinion of your Committee, be made by the Synod of the Province.

F. MONTREAL,
Chairman.

H. GRAHAMSTOWN,
Secretary.

V.

On Declaration of Submission to Regulations of Synod.

Your Committee recommend that, in all branches of the Church, the government of which is not determined by law, a Declaration should be made by those who hold office therein. They consider that a Declaration is necessary, in order to define the conditions of the consensual compact, and that it should be framed so as to secure submission to all synodical action in its legitimate sphere, and to the decisions of the constituted Tribunals.

They recommend the following Declaration to be made, before the Metropolitan, or some person duly appointed by him, by all Bishops elect, either before their consecration, or, if already conse-crated, before exercising any Episcopal functions in their diocese :—

"I, *A. B.*, chosen Bishop of the Church and See of   , do promise that I will teach and maintain the doctrine and discipline of the United Church of England and Ireland, as acknowledged and received by the Pro-vince of   , and I also do declare that I consent to be bound by all the rules and regulations which have heretofore been made or which may from time to time be made, by the Synod of the Diocese of   , and the Provincial Synod of   , or either of them; and, in consideration of being appointed Bishop of the said Church or See of   , I hereby undertake immediately to resign the said appointment, together with all the rights and emoluments appertaining thereto, if sentence requiring such resigna-tion should at any time be passed upon me, after due examination had, by the Tribunal acknowledged by the Synod of the said Province for the trial of a Bishop; saving all rights of Appeal allowed by the said Synod."

They recommend that the following Declaration be made (in addition to the Declaration required by the rules of that Province or Diocese as to doctrine and worship) by persons to be admitted to holy orders, and by Clergymen to be admitted to the cure of souls, or to any other office of trust in the Church :—

" I, *A. B.*, do declare that I consent to be bound by all the rules and regulations which have heretofore been made, or which may from time to time be made, by the Synod of the Diocese of   , and the Provincial Synod of   , or either of them; [and in consideration of being appointed   , I hereby undertake immediately to resign the said appointment, together with all the rights and emoluments appertaining thereto, if sentence requiring such resignation should at any time be passed upon me, after due examination had, by the Tribunal appointed by the Synods of the aforesaid Province and Diocese for the trial of a Clergyman; saving all rights of Appeal allowed by the said Synod]."

(The part in brackets to be omitted when

there is no appointment to a cure of souls, or office of trust.)

Your Committee consider that it must be left to the Province or Diocese to decide whether laymen who are admitted to any office or position of trust should be required to sign a Declaration of the same nature.

G. A. NEW ZEALAND,
Chairman.

H. GRAHAMSTOWN,
Secretary.

VI.

On Provinces and Subordination to Metropolitans.

On this subject your Committee beg to report as follows :—

They are of opinion that the association or federation of Dioceses within certain territorial limits, commonly called an Ecclesiastical Province, is not only in accordance with the ancient laws and usages of the Christian Church, but is essential to its complete organization.

Such an association is of the highest advantage for united action, for the exercise of discipline, for the confirmation of the election of Bishops, and generally to enable the Church to adapt its laws to the circumstances of the countries in which it is planted.

It is expedient, in the judgment of your Committee, that these ecclesiastical divisions should, as far as possible, follow the civil divisions of these countries.

Of the Bishops of these Dioceses thus associated, one, in conformity with ancient usage, ought to be Metropolitan or Primus, the functions and powers of the Metropolitan being determined by synodical action in the Province, except so far as Metropolitical powers are defined by undisputed General Councils of the Church.

It seems to your Committee most in accordance with primitive usage that the Metropolitical see should be fixed, but they do not deem this to be essential. It appears expedient that the Provincial Synod should have the power of changing, when necessary, the site of the Metropolitical see.

Your Committee do not consider it necessary that the election to the Metropolitical see should be conducted differently from the election to other vacant sees; since the Bishops of the Province possess the right of confirming or refusing to confirm any election.

Your Committee strongly recommend that all those Dioceses which are not as yet gathered into Provinces should, as soon as possible, form part of some Provincial organization. The particular mode of effecting this in each case must be determined by those who are concerned.

It is sufficient for your Committee to point out that the steps to be taken for effecting this change are two-fold, since the relations of the Dioceses in Provincial organization, when complete, are formed on the one hand by the subordination of the Bishops of the Province to a Metropolitan, and on the other by the association of the Dioceses in Provincial action. Any alteration of existing arrangements would require, therefore, in the opinion of your Committee, the concurrent action of the Diocese which is to be gathered into a Province with other neighbouring Dioceses, and of his Grace the Archbishop of Canterbury, to whom the Bishops of the Dioceses that at present are extra-provincial have taken the oath of canonical obedience. In the case of the limits of an existing Province being altered, the consent of the Synod of that Province would be required for the alteration.

F. MONTREAL,
Chairman.

H. GRAHAMSTOWN,
Secretary.

VII.

*REPORT of the Committee appointed under Re-
solution XI. of the Lambeth Conference[6].*

Your Committee report that, after full consideration of the questions referred to them by the Conference, they have adopted the following Resolutions :—

I. That every branch of the Church is entitled
to found a Missionary Bishopric.

II. That it is desirable that each branch of the
Church should act upon rules agreed upon before-
hand by the Synod or other Church Council of the
said branch.

III. That each Missionary Bishopric should be
deemed to be attached to one branch of the Church,
and that all rules for the election of a Missionary
Bishop, and for the formation of a Diocese or
Dioceses out of the Missionary District, should be
made by the Synod or other Church Council of
such branch of the Church.

---

[6] RESOLUTION XI.—" That a Special Committee be appointed
to consider the Resolutions relative to the Notification of
proposed Missionary Bishoprics, and the Subordination of
Missionaries."

IV. That notice of the erection of any Missionary Bishopric, and the choice and consecration of the Bishop, should be notified to all Archbishops and Metropolitans, and all Presiding Bishops, of the Anglican Communion.

V. That in appointing a Missionary Bishop, the district within which he is to exercise his Mission should be defined as far as possible; and that no other Bishop should be sent within the same district, without previous communication with that branch of the Church which gave mission for the work.

VI. That, while peculiar cases may occur in Missionary work, owing to difference of race and language, in which it may be desirable that more than one Bishop should exercise episcopal functions within the same district; the Committee consider that such cases should be regarded as exceptions, justified only by special circumstances.

VII. That, with respect to the special case of Continental Chaplaincies, the Committee suggest to the Conference the consideration of some ecclesiastical arrangement by which the various congregations of the Anglican Communion may be under one authority, whether of the English or American Church.

VIII. That the conditions on which a Missionary Bishopric should be brought within a Provincial organization should be—

(1). The request of the Missionary Bishop, addressed both to the Church from which he received mission, and to the Province which he wishes to join.

(2). The consent of the Church from which he received mission, that consent being given by the Metropolitan or Presiding Bishop.

(3). The consent of the Province he wishes to join, that consent being given by the Provincial Synod.

IX. That the status, jurisdiction, and designation of the Bishop thus received into a system of Provincial organization should be determined by the Synod of the Province to which his Bishopric shall be then attached.

X. That, as a general rule, it is expedient that such Missionary Bishopric should be attached to the nearest Province; but that in certain cases it may be necessary that some more remote Province should be selected.

Bishop Tozer's Mission is a case to which the Committee desire to draw the attention of the Conference, as being one in which, for the present, Provincial organization would seem to be impracticable, from the isolation of the district in which Bishop Tozer exercises his episcopal functions, and its remoteness from the Province of South Africa.

XI. That Missionary Bishops and their Clergy

should be bound generally to the Canons of Doctrine and Discipline of the Church from which their mission is derived, or to which they may have been united, and that all alterations in matters of discipline be communicated to the authorities of that Church.

XII. That when a Missionary Church shall be received into the organization of a Provincial Synod, the said Church should be bound by the acts of that body; but that, in order to effect this, the Missionary Church should be granted a power of representation, or of vote by proxy, in such Synod.

XIII. That, as a general rule, in conformity with Church order, all Missionaries and Chaplains residing or engaged in the exercise of ministerial duty within the Diocese or District of a Colonial or Missionary Bishop should be licensed by, and be subject to the authority of, the said Bishop.

XIV. That every Clergyman removing from one Colonial or Missionary Diocese or District into another Diocese ought to carry with him Letters Testimonial from the Colonial or Missionary Bishop whose Diocese or District he is leaving.

XV. That no person admitted to Holy Orders by the Bishop of any Diocese in England or Ireland, who shall afterwards have been serving under the jurisdiction of any Scottish, Colonial, or Foreign Bishop, should be received into any of the Home Dioceses, without producing Letters Dimissory or Commendatory from the Scottish, Colonial, or Foreign Bishop in whose Diocese he has been serving.

XVI. The attention of this Committee has been called to the clause in the Paper of Arrangements for the Conference, headed " Subordination of Missionaries." The Committee has failed to understand what is meant by the words "instructions from those in authority at home," but it can recommend no scheme which interferes with the canonical relation which subsists between a Bishop and his clergy.

W. J. GIBRALTAR,

Chairman.

WILLIAM GEORGE TOZER, MISSIONARY BISHOP,

Secretary.

VIII.

*REPORT of the Committee appointed under Re-
solution VI. of the Lambeth Conference*[c].

By the Resolution of the Lambeth Conference
two questions were referred to the Committee :

I. How the Church may be delivered from a
continuance of the scandal now existing in Natal?

II. How the true faith may be maintained ?

I. On the first question, the Committee recommend that an Address be made to the Colonial
Bishoprics' Council, calling their attention to the
fact that they are paying an annual stipend to a
Bishop lying under the imputation of heretical
teaching, and praying them to take the best legal
opinion as to there being any, and if so what,
mode of laying these allegations before some competent court, and if any mode be pointed out,

[c] RESOLUTION VI.—" That, in the judgment of the Bishops
now assembled, the whole Anglican Communion is deeply
injured by the present condition of the Church in NATAL : and
that a Committee be now appointed at this General Meeting to
report on the best mode by which the Church may be delivered
from a continuance of this scandal, and the true faith maintained. That such Report shall be forwarded to his Grace the
Lord Archbishop of Canterbury, with the request that he will
be pleased to transmit the same to all the Bishops of the
Anglican Communion, and to ask for their judgment there-
upon."

then to proceed accordingly for the removal of this scandal.

The Committee also recommend that the Address to the Colonial Bishoprics Council be prefaced with the following statement:—

"That, whilst we accept the spiritual validity of the sentence of deposition pronounced by the Metropolitan and Bishops of the South African Church upon Dr. Colenso, we consider it of the utmost moment for removing the existing scandal from the English Communion that there should be pronounced by some competent English court such a legal sentence on the errors of the said Dr. Colenso as would warrant the Colonial Bishoprics' Council in ceasing to pay his stipend, and would justify an appeal to the Crown to cancel his Letters Patent."

II. On the second question :

"How the true faith may be maintained in Natal?"

The Committee submit the following Report:—

That they did not consider themselves instructed by the Conference, and therefore did not consider themselves competent, to inquire into the whole case; but that their conclusions are based upon the following facts:—

1. That in the year 1863, *forty-one* Bishops concurred in an Address to Bishop Colenso, urging him to resign his Bishopric.

2. That in the year 1863, some of the publi-

cations of Dr. Colenso, viz.:—" The Pentateuch and Book of Joshua critically examined," Parts I. and II., were condemned by the Convocation of the Province of Canterbury.

3. That the Bishop of Capetown, by virtue of his Letters Patent as Metropolitan, might have visited Dr. Colenso with summary jurisdiction, and might have taken out of his hands the management of the Diocese of Natal.

4. That the Bishop of Capetown, instead of proceeding summarily, instituted judicial proceedings, having reason to believe himself to be competent to do so.

That he summoned Dr. Colenso before himself and suffragans.

That Dr. Colenso appeared by his proctor.

That his defence was heard and judged to be insufficient to purge him from the heresy.

That, after sentence was pronounced, Dr. Colenso was offered an appeal to the Archbishop of Canterbury, as provided in the Metropolitan's Letters Patent.

5. That this Act of the African Church was approved—

By the Convocation of Canterbury;

By the Convocation of York;

By the General Convention of the Episcopal Church in the United States, in 1865;

By the Episcopal Synod of the Church in Scotland;

By the Provincial Synod of the Church in Canada, in the year 1865;

And, finally, the spiritual validity of the sentence of deposition was accepted by *fifty-six* Bishops on the occasion of the Lambeth Conference.

Judging, therefore, that the See is spiritually vacant; and learning, by the evidence brought before them, that there are many members of the Church who are unable to accept the ministrations of Dr. Colenso, the Committee deem it to be the duty of the Metropolitan and other Bishops of South Africa to proceed, upon the election of the Clergy and Laity in Natal, to consecrate one to discharge those spiritual functions of which these members of the Church are now in want.

In forwarding their Report to his Grace the Lord Archbishop of Canterbury, as instructed by the Resolution of the Conference, the Committee request his Grace to communicate the same to the adjourned meeting of the Conference, to be holden at Lambeth on the tenth day of the present month.

G. A. NEW ZEALAND,
Convener.

December 9th, 1867.

IX.

Form of Letters Dimissory for the Clergy.

To the Right Reverend the Bishop, and Reverend the Clergy, and to the faithful in Christ, of the Diocese of A.

We, B., by Divine permission Bishop of C., send greeting in the Lord.

We commend to your brotherly kindness by these our letters, D. E., Priest [or Deacon] of our own Diocese, beseeching you to receive him in the Lord, as a brother, sound in the Faith, of a well-ordered and Religious Life, and worthy of all Christian Fellowship, and to render him any assistance of which he may stand in need; and so we bid you farewell in Christ our Lord.

Witness our hand,

A. Bishop.
B. Secretary.

RESOLUTIONS

ADJOURNED CONFERENCE.

RESOLUTION I.—"That this adjourned meeting of the Conference receives the Report (No. I.) of the Committee now presented, and directs the publication thereof, commending it to the careful consideration of the Bishops of the Anglican Communion, as containing the result of the deliberations of that Committee; and returns the members of the same its thanks for the care with which they have considered the various important questions referred to them."

(The same Resolution was passed with reference to Reports II., III., IV., V., VI., VII.)

RESOLUTION II.—"That the Report (No. VIII.) of the Committee appointed under Resolution VI., laid before this meeting by his Grace the Archbishop of Canterbury be received and printed;

that the thanks of this Meeting be given to the Committee for their labours; and that his Grace be requested to communicate the Report to the Council of the Colonial Bishoprics' Fund."

RESOLUTION III.—"That his Grace be requested, if applied to by the House of Bishops in the Episcopal Church in the United States of America, to allow a copy of the Records of the Conference to be made for them, and to be lodged in the hands of such officer as shall be designated by the House of Bishops to receive it, for reference by Bishops only, but not for publication."

RESOLUTION IV.—" That his Grace the Archbishop of Canterbury be requested to convey to the Church in Russia an expression of the sympathy of the Anglican Communion with that Church, in the loss which it has sustained by the death of his Eminence Philarete, the venerable Metropolitan of Moscow."

RESOLUTION V.—" That the thanks of this Conference be given to the Bishop of Grahamstown for the valuable services which he has rendered as Secretary to many of the Committees appointed by the Conference."

RESOLUTION VI.—" That the thanks of this Conference be given to Philip Wright, Esq., and to

Isambard Brunel, Esq., Barrister-at-Law, for their aid as Assistant Secretaries to the Committees; and especially to the latter for his valuable assistance in all matters that required legal advice."

RESOLUTION VII.—" That we cannot close this Conference without conveying our hearty thanks to his Grace the Archbishop of Canterbury, both for convening this meeting, and for the mode in which he has presided over its deliberations."

Besides the preceding Resolutions,—

The President reported that he had been authorized to annex the following signatures to the Encyclical Letter :—

> A. T. CICESTR.
> AUCKLAND, BATH AND WELLS.
> ROBERT DOWN AND CONNOR.
> WILLIAM DERRY.
> EDWARD NEWFOUNDLAND.
> J. FREDERICTON.
> T. E. ST. HELENA.

2. The following Bishops were appointed as a Sub-Committee, for the purpose of drawing up a Bill, in accordance with a Report submitted by

the Committee appointed under Resolution IX. of
the previous meeting :—

BISHOP OF LONDON,
   „ OXFORD,
   „ LINCOLN,
   „ ELY,   •
   „ . LICHFIELD (Elect),
   „ MONTREAL,
   „ GRAHAMSTOWN,
BISHOP TROWER.

3. His Grace the Archbishop of Canterbury laid
on the table a form of Letters Dimissory [1], which
he had prepared, in accordance with Resolution
II. of the last session of the Lambeth Conference.

4. The Bishop of Illinois, at the request of
the Conference, stated that the Meeting of
the Triennial General Convention of the Protestant Episcopal Church in the United States
would be held on the first Wednesday of Oc-
tober next, in the City of New York; and, in
behalf of the Church in the United States,
offered an affectionate invitation to the Bishops of
the Conference to be present on that occasion ;
and also expressed the hope that the different
branches of the Anglican Communion would
depute one or more Bishops as Representa-

[1] IX. page 39.

tives of the Mother and Colonial Churches, to be present on that occasion, assuring all that might accept this invitation of cordial welcome and affectionate brotherhood.

5. At the request of the Conference, the Bishop of Lichfield (Elect) undertook the office of Corresponding Secretary for the Bishops of the Anglican Communion.

His Grace the President then pronounced the Benediction, and the Conference was closed.

THE END.

GILBERT AND RIVINGTON, PRINTERS, ST. JOHN'S SQUARE, LONDON.

www.ingramcontent.com/pod-product-compliance
Lightning Source LLC
Chambersburg PA
CBHW021439090426
42739CB00009B/1559